FULL POWER PERSUASION SKILLS

Master The Most Effective Methods of Communication Excellence

Alan Mintz

Bloomington, IN   Milton Keynes, UK

authorHOUSE®

AuthorHouse™
1663 Liberty Drive, Suite 200
Bloomington, IN 47403
www.authorhouse.com
Phone: 1-800-839-8640

AuthorHouse™ UK Ltd.
500 Avebury Boulevard
Central Milton Keynes, MK9 2BE
www.authorhouse.co.uk
Phone: 08001974150

First published by AuthorHouse 7/21/2006

ISBN: 1-4259-4565-1 (sc)

Printed in the United States of America
Bloomington, Indiana

This book is printed on acid-free paper.

INTRODUCTION

Congratulations. The fact that you are reading this introduction means that you are at least curious about the process of taking control of your life and possessing the power to achieve your highest goals.

Wait a minute. Doesn't that sound a bit overblown for a book on communication skills? Actually, no. Not if we take an honest look at the skills needed to become a truly effective communicator.

First, you must be able to understand others, to accurately assess their beliefs and viewpoints.

Second, you must be able to relate and collaborate. This means being so self secure that you can easily shrug off your own petty grievances. You can ignore differences between you and others and focus on the larger joint-goal that satisfies everybody.

Third, you are able to speak and present yourself in a way that draws people to you. Others are eager to hear your words. You have the ability to influence, motivate—to change others to your way of thinking.

Now that's a powerful skill.

Psychologists call it Social Intelligence. It is an important gauge of an emotionally stable and fruitful life, a life where you are secure within yourself and productive with others as you confidently march toward your ultimate goals.

In the business world it is a commonly accepted fact that the higher you climb professionally, the more important your interpersonal and presentational skills become. Eventually, if you continue to aspire, these skills become absolutely necessary.

To help you on the road to excellence, I have drawn from the leaders in the top echelons of our society, the premier communication experts—top level executives, CEO's, owners of large industry and, of course, politicians. THEY succeed because they've mastered the keys of human relations and diplomacy.

What they do and how they do it when communicating with others is what I teach in this book. After all, if you want to excel, why not learn from the best.

I shall do my best to keep this book succinct and to the point. Short and sweet and hard to beat as my sixth grade teacher used to say. She didn't like to waste people's time and neither do I. You don't need a lot of preachy motivational type speeches to pad out the book.

What you need and what I offer are the keys to communication mastery. If you practice and learn these skills, you will possess the power to realize your highest aspirations.

TABLE OF CONTENTS

THE STRONGEST FOUNDATION OF COMMUNICATION
    EXCELLENCE 1

CREATING THE COMFORT ZONE 9

POSITIVE INTENT 19

APPRECIATION, VALIDATION AND PRAISE 25

THE OTHER PERSON'S PERSPECTIVE 35

CONFLICT MANAGEMENT
    THE BEST WAYS TO PUT OUT THE FIRES 43

HOW TO HANDLE MISTAKES 51

REMEMBER THE GREEKS 57

SPEAK THE SPEECH 61

CHAPTER ONE

THE STRONGEST FOUNDATION OF COMMUNICATION EXCELLENCE

Every great communicator knows the theory that serves as the best foundation for exceptional communication skills. This foundation is the Humanistic theory of psychology. Several brilliant psychological researchers, such as Abraham Maslow, Eric Frohm and Carl Rogers developed the theory that serves as a flawless blueprint for influencing others. They spent decades researching the most constructive ways for people to relate. Their research spells out the strongest methods that you can use to attract others to you so that your words can be heard, understood and appreciated.

Their years of hard work have given us the perfect recipe for superior interpersonal and presentational skills. The Humanist theory paves the way for us to become top notch communicators because it treats the core issues of personal communication in a positive, proactive and optimistic view that holds the promise of constant personal growth.

Humanistic theory shows us that all of us are built for success. We each have the power to achieve wired into our system, waiting to be used. It is a potential that some people tap into, others do not. It is a conscious choice. If you do realize that achievement and fulfillment can be yours, then you begin to project your success-oriented behavior onto others. Since way down deep others want to succeed, they can only respond positively. Your positive projection has tapped into the same potential that you and everyone has. So an enthusiastic response is only natural; you've given them permission to enjoy the upbeat optimism that waits inside all of us.

LIKE ATTRACTS LIKE

To sum up: A positive success-geared approach to others will fire up the same feelings in them, causing the Humanistic attraction---ears will be opened, your words will be heard and your influence will create its desired effect.

So how do you do this? How do you draw other people into your circle? How do get them to accept your viewpoint? There are two golden keys to creating the positive attitude that acts like a magnet to accepting your point of view.

KEY #1: UNDERSTANDING

People are not cogs in a giant machine. They are not drones or fools to be duped or manipulated. People are individuals, each with their own individual history—and individual potential. Each individual's personality and behavior has been determined to a large extent by their history. All their experiences, family upbringing, neighborhood environment, schooling and so on has formed their outlook. Their history has made them who they are, it has formed their viewpoint. And you must see that viewpoint as VALID. Completely valid.

They didn't ask for it, they didn't pick their viewpoint out of a selection. It came to them through all the outside influences that happened by circumstance, not by choice. Just like you. So how they look at the world is indeed quite valid.

KEY #2: EMPATHY

Let's say you had to work with someone whose point of view was very different from yours. In fact you found them negative, difficult or downright weird. Well, consider this: if you had spent a lifetime walking in their shoes, if you had gone through everything they had gone through, you would feel exactly as they do. You would hold their beliefs and see the world as they see it.

Many might say this is obvious (it is). But few truly give this outlook towards others the depth needed to create this all important connection. Take this empathic stance deeply to heart because this is a crucial step to becoming an effective communicator. If you allow yourself to look at the other person as a human being who has just as much right to their viewpoint as you have to yours, then you've taken a terrific first step.

It doesn't matter if you think their viewpoint is odd, bizarre or flat out wrong. YOU DON'T HAVE TO AGREE BUT YOU DO HAVE TO ACCEPT. Accept their right to their viewpoint and you will have started building the communication bridge, a bridge that will let them walk to you and listen to your words. You will have started the process of shaping their goals to fit yours.

YOUR ATTITUDE DECIDES YOUR BEHAVIOR

When you look at someone objectively and accept them for who they are, your behavior will follow right behind—a positive behavior created by a positive attitude that allows you to rise above any petty grievances or grudges you might hold. No judgment, no bitterness, just a clear eye on accepting who they are for what they are. We're talking about compassion. And what does a person see and hear when greeted with compassion? The words you choose, the tone of voice, your gestures and expressions will all combine into a picture that shows acceptance of their viewpoint. This is validation and everyone needs validation.

Validation is the door at the end of the communication bridge. Validation means you recognize their viewpoint which means you are ready to work with them. You are a collaborator. When you show that kind of positive, open behavior, you develop trust, which is all important. With trust, the other person believes you have THEIR INTERESTS IN MIND—that's what they need if they're going to listen to what you have to say.

GIVE THEM A GIFT

You hand over this proactive desire for collaboration as a gift. You do not force, you do not impose, preach or lecture. You have listened to what they have to say, you acknowledged their right to their viewpoint. Now the other person understands intellectually that you regard them with respect. They feel emotionally that you are a safe ally. Trust then comes freely. The communication bridge is complete.

So to sum up, you are presenting an attitude that appeals to the other person's need for recognition, creating trust that allows them to approach you. You, in turn, will now be able to voice your needs and goals because they see that whatever you say, you have their interests in mind.

If I broke it down into a formula, it would look like this:

COMMUNICATION=LISTENING AND ACCEPTANCE
LISTENING AND ACCEPTANCE CREATES BELIEF
BELIEF CREATES TRUST
TRUST=THEY KNOW YOU HAVE THEIR INTERESTS IN MIND

For the most part, people can only respond positively and appreciatively to this formula. By and large, you'll find yourself facing a helpful comrade who will collaborate towards the achievement of your JOINT-GOALS. And that's the whole point—to create a partnership where they want to work with you and help you meet your goals because you've shown them that you respect theirs.

Of course, I cannot say that absolutely everyone will cross the communication bridge to you. There will always be some real psychopaths, truly evil people who have no qualms with manipulation or abuse. There will always be paranoid people who will treat everything you say with suspicion. Toss them an ounce of pity and move on. Life is too short and you have goals to achieve. The vast majority will respond.

WHAT PEOPLE WANT, WHAT PEOPLE NEED

Carl Rogers' many years of client-centered therapy and research has given us another valuable key to reaching others and allowing them to open up to you. Most people hold near and dear the deep desire to grow and develop in every area of their lives. Rogers tells us that most people hold at their very core the potential to achieve the greatest heights, professionally, personally and spiritually. This ultimate goal is what Abraham Maslow calls self-actualization.

When you tap into that wellspring of desire with a positive intent that shows you have their interests in mind, they will respond in kind. It's a natural reaction. People are waiting for a clear opportunity for growth and change. You are giving them that opportunity when you acknowledge that they are valid human beings. You are fanning their flame. People are waiting for <u>you</u> to give them acceptance so they have permission to climb another rung on life's ladder. People need a reason to move up in their lives and your humanistic validation is a big green light. The most natural reaction is for them to help you do the same—they'll want to keep the collaboration strong, keep working toward the joint goal. Everyone wants to win so why not promote an environment where everyone's a winner?

Ultimately, no sane, reasonable person is stopping YOU from achieving YOUR goals, regardless of how different their viewpoint might be. You are in control of your life, you are the captain of your ship. Everyone wants to think the same about themselves and they are waiting to hear that from you. They WANT you to make the first positive move that will lead them to help you. The potential is there, you just have to recognize it.

Philosophers such as Jean-Jacques Rousseau have known this for centuries. The psychologists of our generation proved it in their research. And the executives, industrialists and politicians know this. The leaders of our country rely on the people-centered theory of humanistic communication to maintain and increase their power.

Over eighty years ago Henry Ford understood the importance of humanistic communication when he said: **"If there is any one secret of success, it lies in the ability to get the other person's point of view and see things from that person's angle as well as your own."**

So now you've got a basic idea of what lies at the core of effective communication. That was the "executive summary" as corporate chiefs like to say. The following chapters will go into detail the different components of communication mastery. I will delve into the nuts and bolts of the influencing techniques used by those that are in power. Do what they do so you can climb the ladder to your highest goals.

If you want to sound good and look good you can learn tricks and gimmicks from some presentation skills coach. But if you want the power to influence others to your way of thinking, then learn from the great communicators. Their strong sense of self gives them the ability to rise above their own petty problems so they can reach out, understand others and show a positive intent. If you do that, the other person will come to you and hear your words.

CHAPTER TWO

CREATING THE COMFORT ZONE

I'd like you to take a look at these potentially nerve-wracking scenarios:

A. You've just started a new job with a company much larger than where you last worked. Your responsibilities are much more extensive than before and your new boss has just called you into his office for an initial meeting where he said he wants to go over "absolutely everything."

B. You've just been promoted to a supervisory position and you need to schedule a meeting to introduce yourself to the team that will be working under you.

C. You've just been assigned a new project at work. The project is big, very important. If you do it well, this will be a big boost to your career. You'll be working with two others on the project who have been transferred from another division. You know nothing about them and you need to be able to count on them completely.

If you're rising in the ranks (or trying to) you are going to find yourself in these type of situations on a regular basis. Face to face encounters where what you say and how you say it will make the difference between being successful and being a loser. The first thing you have to do is create a comfort zone--both for yourself and for the others you're speaking with. You need to quickly create an environment where everyone feels at ease, non-threatened and downright welcomed. Life is a party and you're the host. So let's start with getting you into the comfort zone.

FOCUS OUTWARD, NOT INWARD

To get rid of your own anxiety or defensiveness, you must take your focus outside yourself. You cannot fill your head with any thoughts about how good you look, how professional you're going to appear or any other self-conscious garbage. If you're thinking about how you're going to pull off this meeting or presentation or interview or whatever, that's what they'll see and then the beads of anxiety sweat will start popping out on your brow.

Take your thoughts off yourself, direct your attention towards the others, filled with the intention of creating the communication bridge. Now the burden is off your shoulders. You are involved in the OTHER person. Your thoughts toward the other person leads to actions and words for THEM. You can be comfortable with yourself because you're not presenting for yourself, you're off the hook. This is not about you. You are there to seek out their self-centeredness and avail yourself to them.

Your outward focus must include some simple techniques during those crucial first few minutes of a new interaction. You need to set the groundwork for the collaborative environment right away. They need to sense right away that they can relax, let their guard down. They need to feel that you are available, accessible, respectful and interested in working with what they have to offer. Then you will have created the comfort zone.

Fortunately, there are four basic communication techniques that go a long way in creating the comfort zone very quickly. But to make them work you have to act quickly. Like I said, those first few minutes are crucial. The techniques are simple. You probably already do all four to a certain extent. But if you are deeply aware of these four techniques so that you can maximize them, they become extremely powerful.

BLENDING

Simply put, blending is copying slightly the other person's physicality. This means you observe their major gestures and physical attitude and adjust slightly to create a hint of sameness. Remember, I said slightly. You do not mimic, you do not copy. If you do, you'll look like a weak-kneed idiot.

With blending, you are giving a subtle and generalized adjustment to your gestures that suggests to the other person that you are similar and like-minded. You are a member of their tribe. Once again, I remind you to be very subtle. You accommodate slightly to the gestures that are the most obvious, the ones that the other person uses the most.

For instance, let's say you're meeting with Mr. High Energy, a one man cheerleading squad who constantly paces and slices the air with sweeping arm movements. You don't blend by jumping up and down and waving flags. You do a few occasional gestures that are a just a bit larger than what you would normally do. You stand a few times, take a few steps. The point is that you expand out of your physical frame of reference and show positive intent by showing their physical frame of reference.

What you are doing is relating to the other person on an instinctual, emotional level. You're reaching to the cave man days, way down deep in the limbic system. You are tapping into a person's basic instincts of survival and safety. You are appealing on an emotional level, fulfilling their instinctual, primary need for safety---you are an ally, not an enemy. Everyone still has these basic, prehistoric instincts. Pay attention to these primary urges with a slight blending. You will do a lot towards creating a comfort zone.

PLAYBACK

This is just like a tape recorder where you record something and then play it back to make sure you got it on tape. In communicating, playback means repeating word for word or paraphrasing very closely what the other person just said. You, of course, do not repeat incessantly. You're not a parrot. You choose the key points of a conversation that are the most important. When you playback an important point periodically, you are accomplishing two important communication goals.

First of all, you are making sure you really do understand totally what's being said. This is an obvious point but an important one. Many conflicts are caused by miscommunication, a simple lack of understanding. But that is easily solved by simply repeating what the other person just said. If you didn't get it right the first time, you'll find out immediately. You can move on without embarrassment since the communication gap received an instant repair right in the moment.

Second, every time you repeat a phrase or sentence, you are helping to build that all-important rapport. You are showing the respect and recognition that creates trust. You are letting the other person know that what they are saying is important enough to be said <u>twice</u>. What the other person sees and senses is that you are not contemptuous or superior. They see that you are focused on their words and will appreciate your effort to ensure that everything is crystal clear. Playback is simple but it's a strong nail hammered into the communication bridge.

INQUIRY

There's an old Jewish saying that goes like this: "The only thing better than a good answer is a good question." If you want to obtain information (and I hope you do because you can't respond to what you don't know) there is only one method---inquiry. Asking questions. Ask and then ask some more. The more information you have on the other person's perspective, the more strength you'll have to deal with them. The more you know, the more you can do.

The most effective method of inquiry is the open question. The open question cannot be answered with a yes or a no. The response has to be a full sentence. In other words, you ask a question that demands information, elaboration or explanation. As Rudyard Kipling said, "I had six honest serving men who taught me all I knew. Their names were what and where and when and which and why and who."

Whether you are in sales, human resources or upper management, you need information from the other person. No matter what kind of meeting, planning session or sales presentation you're in, you need to leave no stone unturned. Knowledge is power. The open question works beautifully to give you the information you need.

Let's say you're in a meeting that's coming to a close. You want to make sure that you know as much as you can. You ask an open question, a question that demands a response in the form of a full sentence. A good way to start is to ask for the other person's perceptions or opinions on the topic. Your reward—a piece of information. From that information you can form another question, which leads to more information, which leads to another question and so on. You can keep this going as long as you want, finding out everything you need to know and probably a few things you don't. The open question can perpetually dig into the topic being discussed and unearth every thought, belief and opinion the other person holds.

Once again we have the double benefit of strengthening the interpersonal communication bridge. Using open inquiry shows curiosity, which shows interest in the other person, which shows respect, and that shows the desire to collaborate. The enthusiastic process of open inquiry is another way to reach out with the believability that builds trust. You are holding the other person's thoughts in high regard. They will feel important and everybody likes to feel important. You are venturing into the number one area that most people like to talk about—themselves. Open inquiry allows the other person to talk about that number one topic and feel all the more comfortable with someone who will let them.

LISTENING

Deep, reflective listening is an active skill. True listening is the ability of mental focus where you push aside all extraneous thoughts and totally zero in on the speaker. You use both your ears and eyes because you need to hear the words, sense the tone in their voice and interpret their body and facial gestures. If you truly focus your listening without any of your own mental garbage cluttering your brain, then a wealth of information will come your way.

The problem for many of us, however, is that we don't discipline ourselves to energize our listening and focus on the other person. There are two reasons why we let our listening powers fail us. First, there is the problem of the preconceived notion. As soon as someone starts talking, we immediately start forming an answer in our head. Our insecurities force us to hurriedly slap together an opinion so we'll sound intelligent. It's a defense against our fear of looking stupid. The irony is that since we're so busy trying not to look like an idiot, we run the risk of actually ending up being an idiot.

When you get wrapped up in your own self-centered response instead of focusing on the other person, you miss the whole picture and can only offer a half-baked answer. What you think is an answer is just a rushed attempt to project a slick, professional image.

If you really want to appear slick and professional, then you've really got to listen. Forget about your response. Relax and focus. You don't have to prove anything. You only have to pay total attention to the other person so that you can get the whole picture. You can only give an informed response after you've gotten all the information.

Active listening is a discipline you have to work at. We live in a generation of instant electronic communication, sound-bite journalism and manic media entertainment. We live in fast times that have set our minds for fast results or no results. This is the age of the short attention span. How can you create a calm, focused mind in a world like ours? How can you be consistently attentive in a society designed around the thirty second commercial?

The answer is simple but the process is involved: Practice. Practice makes perfect. You must consciously say to yourself that you will listen. You must observe yourself when your mind wanders into that self-involved playland. You must push your attention back to the other person and keep pushing every time your mind meanders. It's practice, my friend, plain and simple.

The brain is like a muscle. The more you work it, the stronger it becomes. The more you practice focusing your mind, the more focused you become. It demands a constant diligent effort but the pay off is big. The better you listen, the more information you receive. The more information you receive, the more power you have to communicate and attain your goals.

Now I must pause a moment for—The Pause. You would be amazed at how much is accomplished during the few silent seconds of an innocent pause. That brief window between when one person stops talking and other person starts carries a lot of weight for such a small space of seemingly nothing. But the power of the pause is something indeed.

Let's look at the pause in action: John and Bill work at a high prestige, high pressure advertising agency. The politics of keeping clients happy is matched only by the politics of the agency itself. Bill is sitting in John's office and they're brainstorming some ideas before meeting with the whole creative team. John has been with the agency for several years, quite an accomplishment in a profession where the mortality rate is high. Bill is fairly new but is fully aware of the importance of keeping allies and mending disagreements quickly in an ego-driven business.

John just finished describing his view of how the ad campaign should go, giving an overall picture of the theme and how he envisions the print and television ads. Bill doesn't say anything at first. He's smart. He needs John on his side. He knows he needs about eight seconds to help secure the all-important communication bridge before he ventures a response. Bill's eight second performance goes like this: The corners of his mouth turn down in a seriously thoughful frown. His brow furrows in an expression of concentrated thought. Then he slowly nods his head as he emits a low "mmm-hmm". Good job, Bill. You successfully used the power of the pause to accomplish two important tasks.

First, John sensed that Bill doesn't merely respect his opinion, he is also assured that his words are worth serious consideration. John is made to feel worthy. Second, Bill bought himself a few seconds to actually make sure his response was both cohesive and considerate.

Eight lousy seconds can accomplish a lot in establishing rapport and allowing you a window to solidify an intelligent response when intelligence is needed. Behold the power of the pause.

CHAPTER THREE

POSITIVE INTENT

So now you're listening to other people, really listening and showing that you're listening. They've put down their emotional weapons, they're developing trust and are more open to what you have to say. What you say next must build on that trust and solidify the collaborative relationship. If you fall back to pushing, pontificating or any type of hard sell, you'll blow it totally.

You have to stay on track by keeping the following central theme constantly running through your mind:

WHATEVER I OFFER, I DO IT WITH A POSITIVE INTENT GEARED TOWARDS THE JOINT GOAL OF ALL PARTIES INVOLVED.

This is the very essence of masterful diplomacy. If you are focused on the joint goal then everyone will see that you want everyone to be a winner. You're not arguing, you're not debating, you're COLLABORATING. Collaboration is fueled with positive intent and must be the centerpiece of any discussion, planning session, presentation and especially when negotiating conflicts.

Another way to describe positive intent is that you are solution-minded. The words you choose and the way you say them are filled with the intention to find the large scale solution that will affect everyone positively. You are working towards the ultimate goal which is the joint goal.

Here's an example: A manufacturer builds and sells flashlights. Someone in accounting is embroiled in a fight with some of the support staff. Differences in work styles are causing accusations and resentment. Like most conflicts, it stems from petty, ego-based emotions. The supervisor calls them together and begins the diplomatic process. First, the supervisor lets the accountant and the support staff have their say. The supervisor listens and observes, gathering information. Then the supervisor begins her comments by making the following points very clear:

- She is not pinning blame on anyone.
- She wants all the facts of the situation.
- Her desire is only to find a solution that will work for everyone.
- She is confident that there is a solution for everyone

Then comes the centerpiece of positive intent—the joint goal. The big picture. The overall accomplishment that everyone is a part of. The supervisor calmly reminds the arguers that they are not merely employees, they are integral parts of a complex organization. The success of the company depends on them. When the company is successful, they are successful. The company cannot function unless they function together.

Now everyone starts to look at the big picture. The questions that follow are geared towards solutions in light of the big picture.

1. What is your part in making sure those flashlights get on the truck?
2. How can you best accomplish your part of the ultimate goal of getting those flashlights on the truck?
3. What is standing in your way?

From there, all words are focused towards a fact-based, joint-goal solution that keeps the big picture in mind. Infusing your words with positive intent is the smoothest way to deal with different personality types.

A woman who attended one of my communication seminars shared this example: She was the administrative assistant to the dean of a Midwestern college. The dean was a blustery boss, dogmatic and only interested in getting results. He had little patience for process or discussion. One day he burst into the assistant's office and announced that he wanted an extensive re-working of numerous administrative procedures. The assistant sighed deeply. What the dean wanted was extremely involved and would require an enormous amount of organizational work. She would have to coordinate the pool of office staff as if she were a military general in a major war campaign. She was a smart and savvy administrator. She was certainly up to the task. But she also knew this would take time. Concessions would have to be made from other areas in order to get everything done. So here's the problem: How does she appease this blowhard dean and keep him from breathing down her neck?

This is what I told her not to say: "Your orders are extremely involved and difficult to carry out. You'll get what you want but you're going to have to park your fanny and cool your heels. The job will get done but you're just going to have to wait a while--a long while."

This is what I told her she should say: "I totally agree with you. These changes need to be made. I want to make sure everything is done right and meets your expectations. I will organize the secretarial pool and oversee the process every step of the way. This will take at least a month but if I'm allowed the time and space, the results will be excellent. You will have a revamped system to help run this college smoothly exactly the way you want."

Now the second response may have been overdoing it a bit but I wanted her to have plenty of ammunition when presenting her positive intent to deal with the dean. She actually used much of what I suggested and the result left the dean feeling quite content. His ego was appeased. She laid out the situation in a way that would let her get her job done while keeping him happy since everything was said in a positive light geared towards his needs.

Positive intent assures the other person that you are on their side so that they will be comfortable in giving you the breathing room you need.

MODELING

Here is an extremely effective method to induce others to change their behavior to what you want. Modeling is a silent, subtle version of positive intent. In fact, you influence without actually addressing the other person at all.

With modeling, you serve as an example, performing the behavior you want in others. By modeling for others they learn the behavior you want by observation. No preaching, nothing direct. This is influence by inspiration. Modeling is the painless way of inducing change in others when you're struggling with the best way to move a difficult person to your way of thinking. This is a major technique of choice used by countless supervisors, team leaders and managers. They understand the golden rule of trying to change someone: <u>You can't</u>. You cannot enforce change. You cannot convince by imposing your will. No one appreciates a dictator.

When you present an admirable behavior, that is, the behavior YOU want, then the other person is free to simply observe and learn that behavior on their own. There's no scrutiny so it's easier for them to follow their own volition which was inspired by you. If someone sees a behavior that makes sense and will improve their life, more often than not they will be drawn to it and take it for their own. Since there's no obvious effort to push a behavior onto them, then they feel they have freedom of choice. Their learning is risk-free. There's no one judging them, no fear of failure. Modeling is ego boosting for the other person since he or she is making the change themselves. Their new learning comes with a sense of accomplishment because they think they discovered it all by themselves.

School teachers have been using modeling for decades, allowing students to observe, agree and adapt with a feeling of freedom. In this way the teacher is not really a teacher but a facilitator. The student experiences learning as a personal achievement, adding pride and confidence along with the knowledge.

Modeling sits at the center of the Humanist theory—people will respond if you use a positive, validating method to show the benefit of a new idea.

"We are interested in others when they are interested in us"

—Publilus Syrus
Roman Poet, 100 years before Christ

CHAPTER FOUR

APPRECIATION, VALIDATION AND PRAISE

Most people do not merely want to be recognized and validated. They NEED to be recognized and validated. If you want to create open, harmonious communication with other people, then you need to take a little extra time to do the following:

- **Recognize their efforts**
- **Validate their actions**
- **Praise their accomplishments**

Why is it so important to recognize, validate and praise? Because you're helping the other person to feel whole and complete. We're talking about an enormous, deep down need that people have and you're helping to fulfill it.

Alan Mintz

WE ARE WHO PEOPLE SAY WE ARE

Generally speaking, we are social animals. Our daily life is filled with and depends upon interactions with others. More than that, a big chunk of our sense of self is derived from how people accept us. A large part of our identity is formed by the words and actions of others towards us. So when you recognize and validate another person's perspective, their natural reaction is to feel a boost to their self-confidence and a sense of worth. When you can push aside your personal judgments, muster a slight curl of a smile, a small nod of the head, and say, "I can understand where you're coming from", then you've just showed that person that they are accepted as an intelligent and useful human being. It only makes sense that they would respond positively. The other person would relax at a deep emotional level because you've shown yourself to be a like-minded ally. You are satisfying a deep-seated need of acceptance and you will receive acceptance in return.

Let's say you've decided to take some classes in pottery. This is a new venture for you, something to help you de-stress from work. You love the idea of developing a craft and you think you might be good at it. It's now the end of one of your evening classes. You've spent the entire class painstakingly working on one vase. You're covered with splattered clay, your arms feel like they're tied in knots but you're proud of your accomplishment. You think you've made a good vase.

But in order to go on you need to <u>know</u> you've made a good vase. Your efforts need to be validated. You need to

26

know you haven't been fooling yourself. The teacher walks over, looks at the vase and then looks at you. The teacher sees the expectancy in your eyes. Fortunately you've got a teacher who enjoys teaching and knows a few things about human nature. The teacher smiles, complements your work and warmly states that you've got potential. That's all you needed. You breathe a sigh of relief. Your efforts have been accepted. Then the teacher starts tossing some corrections at you, which you hear a lot easier since your identity as an artist has been validated.

I cannot stress enough how important it is to steadily give praise and recognition. This technique is a big gun in your arsenal of collaborative communication excellence. Honest, heartfelt praise can literally change another person. You can actually praise the behavior you want into existence. You can create a belief in someone that turns into reality— the reality you desire.

Maybe I'm starting to sound like one of those pop-psychology motivational gurus. But you know what? It's true.

HOW POWERFUL IS PRAISE? HERE'S THE PROOF

At the beginning of the school year, an elementary teacher was told that she would be given a class of very bright, high achieving students. She was to make sure that these students continue to strive towards excellence. She would teach an advanced curriculum that would best help these upper level students stay on their accelerated track. Moreover, the teacher was told at the beginning of the year that she had been specially chosen to teach these gifted children.

So what do you think happened? The students did very well, of course. The teacher enjoyed a productive year with very few behavior problems, plenty of fast paced learning and high test scores. Now here's the punch line. The teacher was told a huge lie. She and the students were the subjects of a psychological study on expectancy and outcome. In reality, the students were not exceptional high achievers. They were average children chosen at random, no high-end brainiacs. And the teacher was not chosen because of her superior ability to inspire students. Her name was also drawn randomly, out of a hat.

A belief was created for this teacher, a belief that was positive, proactive, praiseful and downright pleasant. The natural human reaction was to accept such a wonderful belief and fulfill the belief by behaving in ways to ensure it really happened.

This example with the teacher and the average class is not an isolated one. Teams of psychologists have performed this study dozens of times at different grade levels. The documented results make it clear as a bell that a positive expectancy can have a powerful effect on creating a positive behavior.

So, the Humanist psychologists have shown us that people possess powerful potentials waiting to be ignited. If you verify that their potentials are alive and active, then the potentials become alive and active. Just as a teacher can create a strong learner, you can create a collaborative and efficient coworker or employee. You really do have the power to create in another person the positive behavior you desire. Remember, most people <u>want</u> to improve, they <u>want</u> to better themselves. They're just waiting for someone to tell them that they are better. They need that validating green light that you can give them. They're waiting for you to give them the permission to become the person you both want them to be.

POSITIVE REINFORCEMENT

Let's assume you've been reading this book avidly, soaking up every word like a sponge. You are aware that you have the power to create a positive behavior in others. You've got an employee with some good points and some bad points. The good points help make the work world go smoothly. The bad points make you want to blow his brains out. You ignore your own petty frustrations and on a fairly regular basis you give that employee some sort of upbeat compliment. You never let more than a few days go by without serving up some sort of acknowledgment or recognition. You are using positive reinforcement.

Positive reinforcement is a ridiculously simple concept. It's easy to learn, easy to use. This is an amazingly effective tool in creating harmony, building allies, and turning people into receptive collaborators who will listen to your words with respect.

If you want clinical proof, just look at the work of psychologist B. F. Skinner. He based his whole career on reinforcement. Skinner became famous for his studies on changing people's behaviors through positive or negative reinforcement. He called his theory operant conditioning. In a nutshell, operant conditioning works like this:

- **Expose someone to a repeated stimulus and their behavior will change.**
- **A positive stimulus will promote the behavior you want.**
- **A negative stimulus will erase the behavior you don't want.**

Skinner performed extensive studies where he used his conditioning techniques to create the behavior he wanted. I know that sounds a little diabolical, like a B-grade sci-fi film with the demented scientist and his mind molding machine, but who cares? Skinner's work is proven. You've got a terrific (and easy) tool to create a harmonious and communicative environment. I only hope that your intent is positive and your goals honorable.

You can find variations of positive reinforcement everywhere. Eastern style meditators use a repeating mantra to raise their mind to a higher spiritual plane. Many motivational leaders teach people to repeat personalized affirmations to create a healthier lifestyle. Athletic coaches totally depend on positive reinforcement to build confidence in their players and teachers use it constantly to encourage their students.

It's hard to believe that you could change yourself or others so effectively with a method as childishly simple as positive reinforcement. But it's true. By regularly offering people positive, complimentary boosts, they will gradually respond by improving in the area you desire.

Here are the two main components of positive reinforcement:

1. **BE AWARE WHEN AN ACCOMPLISHESMENT IS MADE**

   Don't hesitate when the other person has completed a task and done it well. Compliment them right then and there, in the moment. It doesn't have to be anything grand or earthshaking—the report was corrected, the machine repaired, the calls were made, the bills paid, etcetera. As long as they finished something or performed a job in a satisfactory manner, then in that moment make sure you recognize their effort and achievement. You don't have to get obsessive about this and check off your required three compliments for the day in your filofax. Just keep looking past your nose. If you're paying attention, then you'll notice those small achievements that inevitably occur every once in awhile. So maybe once a week or a few times a month the other person receives a positive, identity affirming message. Gradually but steadily you will be boosting their energy, their outlook and their productivity.

2. **DON'T WAIT FOR AN ACCOMPLISHMENT TO HAPPEN**

   Remember, you can create a new behavior in someone by praising that behavior into existence. Just like the story about the teacher who thought she had a class of high achievers. Communicate openly and regularly to the other person a strong confidence that he or she will do the job well. The message will soak in eventually and they will start doing what you have been predicting. The positive reinforcement will gradually take hold, creating what you need from the other person.

What does positive reinforcement sound like? Try this on for size: Let's say your assistant is thorough but tediously slow. It's Monday and you need an assignment finished by Friday. Forget about your typical boss command like "I'll need it by Friday. Have it done by then." Commands don't help.

Instead, try this: "I'm glad you got a good head on your shoulders because I need this by Friday. I'm sure you can pace this out to stay on track." With a positive projection you will greatly increase the chance of having that assistant move closer to the behavior you want. Of course you're a smart and savvy boss so you'll also check in at midpoint, monitor progress and adjust priorities if needed.

There is a hard core, deep down reason why I am making such a strong pitch about all this validation and praise. The reason is this: Most people love to feel important. And feeling important is, well, very important. When you feed others a steady diet of compliments for jobs well done along with positive projections for the future, you are fueling their much needed sense of importance. I don't mean importance in a selfish and egotistical way. I mean importance as in feeling successful, secure and open to improvement.

This sense of importance equals self-esteem. That's what you're helping to give the other person. You will win big time. You will win trust and appreciation—two big bricks in your communication bridge.

So I'll say it one last time. Most people naturally want to improve, they want to increase their abilities and enrich their lives. They want the skill to relate and collaborate with you. But they won't rise up unless they get the big go-ahead from you. They need to hear that it's okay to move on. Tap into that need and you will have the power to influence other's behavior through appreciation, validation and praise.

As John Dewey, the brilliant father of progressive education said:

> *"The deepest urge in human nature is the desire to be important."*

CHAPTER FIVE

THE OTHER PERSON'S PERSPECTIVE

You've probably gathered by now that superior communication does NOT include preaching, pontificating, directing, ordering, demanding or any other mudslide of words used to describe how you can impose your will on others.

If you want people to hear your words and follow what you want, you cannot force yourself upon them in any way. Otherwise, the coveted communication bridge turns into a brick wall. You have to reach out to their world, walk in their shoes and see through their eyes. I touched on this earlier but now let's look at this idea in more detail. First, remember the basic formula:

COMMUNICATION=LISTENING AND ACCEPTANCE
LISTENING AND ACCEPTANCE CREATES BELIEF
BELIEF CREATES TRUST
TRUST=THEY KNOW YOU HAVE THEIR BEST INTERESTS IN MIND

When you accept another person's point of view, you are proving yourself to be an ally—a collaborator who only wants to help. The other person will then intellectually understand that he or she can be open with you and believe your words when you talk. But on the emotional level he or she will feel the basic instinctual sensation of safety and trust. Trust—that's the bottom line in the formula.

As I said earlier there are two important points to keep in mind when it comes to other people's viewpoints:

- **YOU DON'T HAVE TO AGREE**
- **YOU DO HAVE TO ACCEPT**

You accept because their viewpoint is the result of their life experiences that formed their personality. If you had been through what they've been through, you probably would've ended up just like them. They've earned their viewpoint just as you've earned yours. Accept their viewpoint and you'll gain their trust.

Earlier, I talked about the work of Carl Rogers and his client-centered therapy. The work Rogers did in developing effective therapy techniques has turned out to be the greatest prize for anyone who wants to be a master at influencing others. Roger's work may have started as a therapeutic tool for treating emotional problems, but knowledge of its effectiveness spread into all corners of society. The techniques are used to solve intercultural tensions and diplomatic conflicts. Teachers use client centered techniques in the classroom and enjoy fantastic results. Top level business executives and politicians follow Rogers (and the other humanists for that matter) to maintain control in human relations and energize their presentational skills.

This humanistic, person-focused communication technique is <u>the</u> proven way to gain someone's trust, to get them to relax and accept what you have to say. At the beginning of this book I touched upon the key concept of this technique. Now let's look at it in detail.

EMPATHY—THE POWER TO UNDERSTAND OTHERS

Rogers explains it best: "An empathic understanding is by all means the most helpful. Even the intent to understand can itself be of value. Realizing that someone is trying to understand his statements both encourages him to communicate more of himself and also helps him to realize that he… is worthwhile."

Sounds great, but how do you start? How do you begin becoming an expert communicator with this deep empathic power? Here's the first thing you have to do. It's also the most important. If you do this, the rest follows naturally— <u>LISTEN! OPEN YOUR EARS, SHUT YOUR MOUTH AND LISTEN.</u>

Earlier I spoke of the importance of active, focused listening skills. Well, to understand someone's point of view you have to hear it and hear it completely. You listen to the words, the tone, the inflection and the volume. You absorb the quality. You observe the gestures, body posture and facial expressions. Finally, you allow yourself to blend in with all of it. That's true listening. Don't let that scare you. Look at it this way: The more you let them talk, the more information you're getting. That's for you. The more information they give, the more comfortable they become. That's for you, too.

So at first the only things you say are brief words of encouragement, validation or curiosity. You want to induce them to talk more. You don't need to comment very much. You don't need to give your personal opinions. What you need to do is LISTEN.

No judgments. Just accept the viewpoint that they have earned and are entitled to. Make an effort to walk in their shoes. Remember, if you had been through everything they've experienced, you would probably feel the same way. The more you empathize, the more you will win their respect and you will gain a better idea of what to say when it's time for you to talk. Michael Eisner, who was CEO of the Walt Disney Corporation said, "No matter what business you are in, you are dealing with interpersonal relationships. You need an appreciation of what makes people tick."

IT'S NOT ABOUT YOU

Being able to see through someone else's eyes without judgment demands that you pull yourself up above any petty arguments or contempt that's rolling around in your head. You have to have a strong sense of self esteem. You have to keep your eye on the big picture, the joint-goal. Stay above the fight so that your emotional teakettle won't boil over if their viewpoint runs against your grain. As Carl Rogers said, "You must lay aside yourself, and this can only be done by a person who is secure enough in himself that he knows he will not get lost…and can comfortably return to his own world when he wishes."

Fortunately, self esteem is an arbitrary measurement scale that you contrive to measure your self worth. Ultimately, you decide how good you feel about yourself. You're the captain of your own ship. If you are intelligent enough to read this book then you have all the necessary powers to raise your self esteem to the stars. Self esteem is not governed by a level of achievement. High self esteem is a reflection of your desire to grow towards that achievement. Your growth will depend on your acceptance of others.

So let them talk. You can afford to listen. The more you listen, the more you learn. The more you learn, the better you can relate. The more you relate, the more they will relax and trust you. Then everyone's self esteem gets a boost.

As Alfred Adler, one of the great Humanist psychologists said:

> **"It is the individual who is not interested in his fellow men who has the greatest difficulties in life and provides the greatest injury to others. It is from among such individuals that all human failures spring."**

LET THEM THINK IT'S THEIR IDEA

Here's an extra handy tip that goes along with using another's point of view. Instead of pushing your own idea, arrange your comments in a way that will guide them to come up with it themselves. The easy way to do this is to simply ask their opinion if something will work. Or, give them a list of options, saying that you can't decide and you need their input. You of course already know what you need to know. But if you let the other person take charge, he or she will give you what you need on a silver platter as opposed to you trying to convince them.

I learned this during my younger and more vulnerable years. I was working as an actor in New York. I lived the typical artists life—one month I would be performing in a magnificent production in a 1000 seat auditorium and the next month I would be working as a party clown to pay the rent. When I landed a supporting lead in a large musical slated for Broadway, I thought I had it made. The script needed some polishing, but I had confidence in the director. He was a seasoned veteran who would steer us to stardom.

Boy, was I wrong. The director was skittish, neurotic and insecure. During out of town tryouts the show was floundering. We were sinking fast and the director was starting to have a meltdown. Every day he came in with massive script changes that either made no difference or made the show worse. I hated the directions he was giving me. I knew totally how to perform my scenes but trying to tell him would be suicide. An older character actor in the show saw my predicament and gave me this sage advice: "At the next rehearsal tell him there are two ways of doing the scene. One is the way you want to do it, the other is a stupid choice. Show him both. Tell him you're really lost and you need him to decide."

So that's exactly what I did. The neurotic director of course chose the way that made sense. I got to do the scene the way I wanted and he believed the scene went well because of his directorial skill. We were both happy. That's how I handled it for the rest of the rehearsal process. He retained his dignity and I gave the performance I knew was best.

CHAPTER SIX

CONFLICT MANAGEMENT
THE BEST WAYS TO PUT OUT THE
FIRES

Just what is a conflict? Equally important, what is the core reason for most conflicts? Here is a clinical definition that you'll find in a dozen different textbooks:

CONFLICT IS THE PERCIEVED DIVERGENCE OF INTEREST BETWEEN TWO PARTIES WHERE BOTH PARTIES BELIEVE THOSE INTERESTS CANNOT BE ACHIEVED SIMULTANEOUSLY.

The two key words in that definition are PERCIEVE and BELIEVE. Conflict is based on a perception. The individual, subjective viewpoints of the people involved are defining the conflict. The conflict is based on what they think, what they perceive---not necessarily what they

43

know. So at the very core, conflict is based on an emotional reaction. You think you're being held back by your boss, you feel the other person is hindering your job, you believe you can't get finished because of that co-worker, and so on.

If conflict is ultimately based in emotions, then what's the opposite? What is life without conflict? What sort of communication would people practice to create a world free of conflict? Here's the answer:

FACTS—COLD HARD FACTS

The fact finding mission is the cure for conflicts. The more you pay attention to the objective facts surrounding a situation, the less you are dealing with a person's individual perceptions. Stick to the facts and you will rise above any cloudy, personality laden opinions. The fact finding mission will allow you to zero in on the actual events.

This fact finding mission is also known as the solution oriented process. When you are focused on a solution oriented process, you keep your distance from all of the negative garbage that could warp your judgment. You stay above the anger, the bitter accusations and frustration that are wrapped up in individual emotions. You are only concerned with gathering cold, hard factual data. You are on the hunt for a solution, and a solution can only be found through information. Remember, information is power. You commit yourself to information gathering. Your only interest is to find out the actual, real reasons that are causing the log jam.

You have to keep a mind-set that no one is at fault, no one is to blame. You are not dealing with people--you are dealing with a situation. You are on a fact finding mission. The more you focus on gathering facts, the less involved you will be in the emotional spider's web of individual perceptions (including your own). If you stick to the solution process, then you can't get caught up in the angry quagmire of conflict.

From the Comprehensive Textbook of Psychiatry we learn this: "All organisms, including human beings, are incapable of engaging in two incompatible responses at once." There's no place for a fight to grow if you are completely involved only in finding a solution through the fact finding mission. Stick to the mission and the others will have a hard time continuing with the emotional conflict.

Now I admit that the solution oriented process is a tactical and calculated series of maneuvers. But ultimately it's humanistic as well. After all, you're working at creating an environment of harmony. In the final analysis isn't that what everyone wants? (At least the sane ones)

THE STEPS OF THE SOLUTION ORIENTED PROCESS

1. RECOGNIZE AND ACCEPT THEIR POINT OF VIEW
   You validate their right to their opinion, regardless of how nutty it is in order to establish trust.

2. EXPRESS POSITIVE INTENT

You are not interested in a fight. You only want to find a solution with their best interests in mind. You are trying to get a clear idea of the big picture and where everyone fits in.

3. THE FACT FINDING MISSION

    Use questions that include a lot of open inquiry (questions that can't be answered with a yes or no). With each piece of information, maintain objectivity. You are not there to judge. You are there to solve. Stay focused, practice active listening and clarify everything. Backtrack often. You want to make sure you understand. You cannot move on to #4 unless you are confident you have all the information.

4. SOLUTION PROPOSALS

    What you offer is geared for the joint goal because ultimately all parties really are working towards the same unified end.

What I am about to explain next will help you develop a smooth blanket of compassion so that you can graciously work through the solution oriented process. First off, you must remember that normal people develop in stages. As we grow up, we master our life skills one step at a time. After learning one level, we use what we've learned as a spring board to help us get to the next higher level. It doesn't matter what theory of psychology you subscribe to—Freud, Maslow, Erickson, whoever—they all agree that our development occurs in stages.

But what if things go wrong at one of those stages of development? Let's take the example of a teenage boy named Jimmy. His family keeps moving from town to town. Jimmy never gets the time needed to make friends, to find a group of peers that he can hang out with. Unfortunately, it's during the adolescent stage that people learn how to socialize and relate with others. The teenage years are when you learn to feel comfortable with others and feel comfortable about yourself.

Jimmy never had the chance to develop that skill. But time marched on, Jimmy grew up. The people skills and self esteem that he was supposed to struggle with and hopefully develop just didn't happen, there was no chance.

We flash forward fifteen years. Jimmy is now James and works with a large software company. He's a hard worker, very detailed oriented. In fact he's extremely detail oriented. He focuses on being exact, precise and strives for perfection. He doesn't talk much, doesn't socialize and prefers to work on his own. "If you want to do something right, do it yourself" is his motto.

But there are meetings and discussions on a regular basis. He's quiet and rarely contributes. When he does, his responses are short and spoken in a low monotone. He comes off as aloof. People think he's constantly angry so working with him on a project can be unnerving. Others hate it when they have to consult with him.

But down deep James is not surly or angry. He's scared. He never learned how to relate as an adolescent. A building block in his development was missing. The gap left him with an insecurity that he had to cover up with a defensive behavior. James had a developmental deficit. His behavior was an attempt to compensate in the only way he knew how to get through the workday with people. Some call it a defense mechanism, others may call it a complex or condition.

Whatever name you attach to his behavior, it is of the utmost importance that you see James as a human being who has been short changed and needs help. When you encounter someone with a difficult behavior, what you are seeing is someone who got cheated somewhere in their developmental ladder. They're imperfect, incomplete and are doing the best they can with what they've got.

The more of a pain in the neck a person is, then the more he or she is suffering from a developmental deficit. If you look at them that way, then your own frustration factor will drop enormously. A mood of compassion and perhaps a little pity will help you rise above your own shortcomings as you put their behavior into perspective.

Such an attitude of compassion is difficult to swallow when the other person is a raging, abusive creep. But fighting fire with fire rarely works. You need to stay calm and, in turn, calm them down by first saying to yourself:

"SOMEWHERE ALONG THE LINE THAT POOR FOOL GOT CHEATED. HE/SHE DESERVED BETTER THAN WHAT THEY GOT BUT MAYBE I CAN HELP."

The attitude and behavior that follows a statement like that will be noticed. I guarantee it. Especially in a conflict situation. It will be noticed and it will be welcomed. Compassion for another's problem behavior will help clear the air of resentment and allow the solution process to do its job.

> *"If you argue and rankle and contradict, you may achieve a victory sometimes; but it will be an empty victory because you will never get your opponent's good will."*
>
> *—Benjamin Franklin*

CHAPTER SEVEN

HOW TO HANDLE MISTAKES

Everybody messes up eventually. Nobody enjoys pulling a bonehead mistake and nobody enjoys having that bonehead mistake pointed out to them. But when someone fouls up, the mistake has to be dealt with. Fortunately, the two-step responses I give below will help put out the emotional fires that mistakes can cause. You will quickly smooth over ruffled feathers and probably even strengthen your relationship with the other person.

WHEN THEY ARE RIGHT

Okay, you messed up. You can't get around it. You can't cover it up (and shouldn't anyway). The other person just got done pointing out your slip-up. Maybe they were angry, maybe they were preachy and took a holier than thou attitude. It doesn't matter. What matters is that you respond immediately with the following two comments so that you can move on with a minimum of discomfort. Your two steps are:

1. THANK THEM. That's right, you are going to nod your head, muster up some sort of smile and graciously thank them for pointing out your mistake. Shove whatever pride or ego issues you may have on the back burner. Be honest with yourself. You <u>did</u> mess up and quite frankly the other person is doing you a favor by pointing it out to you. Thank them for the opportunity, yes, the opportunity to improve yourself-- to look at the mistake, correct the behavior that created the mistake and become a better person from the experience.

2. REASSURANCE. You next tell them that the mistake won't happen again. You've gotten the information you need to now follow the correct path. You can't make the mistake again because now you have learned what you need to know to avoid this mistake in the future.

This simple two-step response will greatly help resolve the incident and close the case so you can move out of an uncomfortable situation and get on with your life.

What you are doing is turning a negative into a positive. The situation is now one of improvement. You've learned some new information and you're going to use it to be better at your job. That's the long and short of it. Plus, your graciousness and speed won't leave any room for lingering ill will. If you are dealing with one of those judgmental ogres who love to beat people over the head with their righteous indignation, then the fast and gracious thank you will nip them in the bud. Your response is civilized and positive. Stating that you've learned a new improvement erasing the possibility of future mistakes leaves no room for them to drag it out. In 3-4 sentences and maybe 30 seconds you will have covered the bases. Then move on.

WHEN YOU ARE RIGHT

Ah, now the shoe is on the other foot. You are in the right, you are on top, you are in the driver's seat. Well, don't let it go to your head. Don't turn into that judgmental ogre spewing "I'm right, you're stupid" venom. If you play your cards right by practicing a little humane behavior, this can be a golden moment to gain extra power. It's a chance for you to boost collaborative communication and strengthen an ally who will help you when you need them.

After you tell them (in a calm voice, of course) where they made their mistake, you follow up with these quick two steps:

1. EMPATHY. You've got to let them off the hook a little bit. You need to let them know that you are not going to reproach them. You are not going to hold this mistake against them or indulge in any other kind of maliciousness. You have to let them know that they made an honest mistake that could've happened to anyone—it could've happened to you. All it takes is a simple statement of empathy such as: "I can see how you would've made that mistake", or, "I understand why you made that choice."

Whatever insecurities they may have will be immediately taken care of. If they are prone to resentful backlashes—that will be erased. They will be grateful to see that they haven't lost any prestige in your eyes. Moreover, they'll know that you are on their side. By showing empathy, they won't fear coming to you with a question BEFORE a mistake has been made.

2. <u>TOLERANCE</u>. Your second sentence is "Let me know if I can help you avoid mistakes in the future." Please understand that you're not taking responsibility for them. But you are offering input if they want to improve their performance. With that, you've nailed down a strong sense of helpfulness and open communication. At a moment when the other person is in a vulnerable position, you've let them know that they can trust and confide in you. The other person will breathe a sigh of relief and look at you as a true comrade because of your tolerance.

You can well afford to be generous when someone else has made the mistake. After all, you're in the power position. You're right, they're wrong. You both know it and it's pointless to extend that fact any further. What makes excellent sense is to use this moment to show understanding. You will generate another of those positive responses that you need to keep the communication bridge open.

CRITICISM KILLS

The evil twin brother of positive reinforcement is criticism. Criticism is the exact opposite of validation or recognition.

Criticism is negative, harsh, insulting and destroys a person's self esteem.

Since communication is a two way street, the person you angrily criticize could very possibly throw that mood right back in your face. You get what you give. The other person may hide their reaction and keep it bottled up only to have it spew out later, venting their pent up anger in some destructive manner. Whenever and however the backlash occurs, the result is the same. You end up splattered with the same hateful energy that you gave with your criticism.

Think about what you are actually saying when you criticize someone. You are saying that he or she is inferior, incomplete and incompetent. You are vilely telling them they don't have what it takes to get the job done.

So let's exercise a little common sense here. How do you suppose someone will react when you criticize? What kind of response can you possibly expect when you shoot them down with words that negate their efforts and deny their intelligence?

The fallout may be subtle. Perhaps you will have created a silent enemy who quietly keeps their distance, no longer approachable and will gladly let you twist in the wind when you need assistance. Or perhaps the person is a little more vindictive and will slander you in a campaign of whispers behind your back to whoever will listen. Or maybe you prefer a stronger personality, someone whose defensiveness allows them to react with an outright shouting match, throwing the blame right back at you. Whatever their personality, however they react to stress, criticism will make sure it won't be good.

Criticism destroys good will and good will is the glue that holds the communication bridge together. The phrase "constructive criticism" is a contradiction in terms. Criticism can only break down, never build up. If you want someone to change, then you have to positively point them in the direction towards improvement.

If someone really messed up and caused a minor catastrophe, then go back to the fact finding mission. Analyze the steps that led to the mess up. That sort of backtracking will help make sure the same mistakes don't happen again. But finger pointing criticism has no place in communication. It will not help, it will only clog the quality control process with hatred.

So the golden rule is:

DON'T POINT OUT THE FACT THAT THEY WENT WRONG. POINT THEM IN THE DIRECTION OF HOW TO GO RIGHT.

CHAPTER EIGHT

REMEMBER THE GREEKS

The need to develop effective communication tools that can influence others has been around a long, long time. Two Greek philosophers developed some valuable techniques a couple of thousand years ago. They work just as good today, if not better.

SOCRATES AND THE YES QUESTION

Socrates brilliantly thought up a short and simple technique to lead others to your way of thinking. And it works great. All you do is ask the other person a series of questions that can only be answered in the affirmative. Each question you ask is connected in some way to the topic that you want them to agree to. Even if the connection is remote, that's okay. The connection may be small, but if it demands a yes answer, then the person is pushed another step closer to an agreement with you. Keep going with the yes answers and eventually the process will give you your goal—a final total agreement.

ARISTOTLE'S RHETORIC

Aristotle wrote his nifty guidebook entitled Rhetoric some 2,500 years ago. Today it is still a wonderful source for those who want to master positive and ethical interaction. Anyone involved in politics or high-end business negotiations has probably read this at one point or another. At the foundation of Rhetoric there are three terms which are outlined for you below:

ETHOS

This is your reputation, the opinion that others hold about you. Aristotle stressed the importance of others looking at you with trust and respect. The higher their regard, the more power you will have to persuade. If your business relationships are in choppy waters, you may have to beef up your ethos. Aristotle, like so many others after him, considered this of primary importance, since others won't let you state your case unless you have first earned their respect.

PATHOS

This is your awareness of the needs and emotions of the people you are communicating with. Pathos is the ancient forerunner of chapter five in this book—the section on other people's point of view. Aristotle goes deeply into being sympathetic and ultimately empathetic. He stressed that your proposals must revolve around the needs of others.

LOGOS

This refers to the actual words you use—your comments, proposals and ideas. Your words must be used to reach the best possible conclusion for everyone concerned. This is the basis of diplomacy or the big picture that I spoke of earlier. Logos goes far beyond mere compromise. Compromise is a give and take where everyone is only a partial winner. Aristotle urged that we strive for the "greater good" as he called it, which is a consensus. A consensus seeks to benefit everyone in a grander design. Aristotle's idea of consensus is to focus on the overall long term rewards that are superior to the mutual sacrifices of compromise.

CHAPTER NINE

SPEAK THE SPEECH

The higher you climb the corporate ladder, the more you will speak in front of groups. Your life will be filled more and more with instructional trainings, progress report speeches, debriefings, motivational pep talks, keynote addresses—talk, talk, talk. If you want to succeed at the managerial and executive level, then get used to the fact that presentational speaking will be a regular responsibility.

It's no surprise that there is a whole industry of trainers, coaches and seminar leaders who specialize in teaching presentational skills. They're easy to find. Go online to any search engine, type in "public speaking training" and you'll find dozens of seminar companies and consultants. They confidently sell these workshops and seminars because they've seen the numerous surveys informing us that the fear of public speaking is one of the top five fears among Americans—it's actually placed above the fear of death.

Taking a course in public speaking is certainly helpful. Practicing the physical tools of eye contact, gestures, facial expressions, body language and vocal inflection will raise your comfort level. Learning how to structure a speech will give you a sense of control and confidence.

Take some classes or attend some seminars if you feel you need to. But underneath all the tools of speaking, you will need a single all encompassing technique that will motivate your speaking. You will need a foundation that will provide the fuel to make your words convincing. This entire book stems from that one technique that will provide the basis of effective speaking. Everything you've read so far is in some way closely connected to that one theory—The Humanist Theory. This chapter, at its essence, is no different.

COMMUNICATION IS CONNECTION

Remember, the human connection is all important. The listener must feel that you have their best interests in mind; that will allow them to cross the bridge and hear your words. It doesn't matter if you are speaking intimately to one person or an informal talk to a group of five or a formal speech to five hundred. Your underlying reason to speak is the same: to connect on an emotional level. It is on the emotional level that true communication occurs.

I seriously doubt that a supervisor, manager or executive would want to deliver a generalized, meandering speech that has some hazy, roundabout relevance to the business at hand. Of course not. What every speaker wants and needs is a clear cut, well defined reason for giving that speech. There always has to be a singular, definite purpose.

Ultimately, at the very core of every speech that purpose is always the same. Whatever the content, whether it's a sales proposal or an instructional lesson, the speaker's bottom line goal is to make that emotional connection.

What can show your listeners that you are reaching out to make the emotional connection? It can be summed up in the three words below:

THE SHARED BENEFIT

Every great actor knows about motivation. Motivation is the key reason for saying what you are saying. It is the WHY. Why should I say this? What do I want to accomplish by speaking these words? The actor gives an impassioned speech to rally the troups before they go to battle or win his freedom from a life in prison or gain the love of a woman he adores. The purpose of your speech may not be filled with such life and death drama but your motivation is just as important. And what is your motivation? The shared benefit.

The shared benefit means simply that you have discovered something that has made your life better and you now want to share it with others to make their lives better. Whatever you are talking about—a software program, sales technique or office procedure—you are making your listener's lives better. What you know has made your life better and now you're going to make their life better. In return you will earn their respect and admiration. The environment you work in will improve because of what you've said. You will be promoting your career and increasing the chances of advancement because you are selflessly aiding those around you with your discovery. THAT is the shared benefit.

The shared benefit is a powerful motivation that will fuel your words with enthusiasm and the desire to connect emotionally. Remember, people will listen with trust if they believe that you have their best interests in mind. So when preparing a speech, try saying to yourself a few of these motivators to energize your words with the power to draw people to you:

- **I've discovered a secret. I've decided to share it with you because I know you'll love it as much as I did.**
- **My life is so much better now. If you know what I know, your life will be better too.**
- **You want to hear what I have to say, you're waiting for it. Okay, I'll give it to you, only because you want it so bad.**
- **You need what I have. To deny you my knowledge would be cruel.**
- **If you listen to my words, we can all succeed, and we all want to succeed.**

When your motivation is to share a benefit that will improve other's lives that will in turn improve yours, then you will super-charge your words with the magnetic power of humanism.

This is the end of my advice on how to strengthen your ability to communicate effectively. But I hope this short manual will serve as the beginning of a path to success through the power of communication excellence. Remember the formula of winning people to your way of thinking:

THEY WILL LISTEN BECAUSE THEY BELIEVE YOU

THEY WILL BELIEVE YOU BECAUSE THEY TRUST YOU

THEY WILL TRUST YOU BECAUSE THEY KNOW YOU HAVE THEIR BEST INTERESTS IN MIND

****

About The Author

Over the past fifteen years, hundreds of corporations and businesses have benefited from the dynamic seminars and presentations of Alan Mintz. With a background that combines educational theory, psychology and theatre, his programs smoothly blend practical techniques with an entertaining style that makes learning both easy and meaningful. Sales staff for companies ranging from pharmaceuticals to sports gear have honed their speaking abilities through Mr. Mintz's power presentational skills seminars. He also has several years experience teaching diplomatic communication skills, giving managers and supervisors effective techniques to solve conflicts and change difficult personalities into positive performers.

Mr. Mintz's varied experience fuels his seminars and presentations with a special blend of humor, humanity and business savvy. He originally trained as an actor at the Juilliard School and performed on Broadway, several touring productions, film and television commercials. Early in his acting career, he made use of his energetic style by performing at trade shows and corporate promotional events. He so enjoyed the world of business theatre that he eventually created his own company, marketing and creating customized sales presentations. With a dramatic flair he has been able to give many corporations a unique, theatricalized presentation that stood out from the normal promotional fare. Clients were so impressed with his presentations that he was requested to work with sales staff on strengthening communication skills and sales techniques.

Because Mr. Mintz is a licensed teacher with a Master's degree in education, he knows how to work with different learning levels and teach quickly, thoroughly and in a participatory style that energizes and inspires. The business world now enjoys a two-fold benefit from Mr. Mintz's skills: as an insightful teacher of exceptional communication and diplomacy along with the sharp performer's expertise for business promotion.

Currently, he is a full time instructor with American Family Insurance, sharing his abilities in their agent and staff training program.

www.ingramcontent.com/pod-product-compliance
Lightning Source LLC
Chambersburg PA
CBHW022133170526
45157CB00004B/1863